My Journey to
Emotional Healing

My Journey to
Emotional Healing
ONE SMALL STEP AT A TIME

SABRINA CAMMACK

XULON PRESS

Xulon Press
2301 Lucien Way #415
Maitland, FL 32751
407.339.4217
www.xulonpress.com

Unless otherwise indicated, Scripture quotations taken from the Holy Bible, New International Version (NIV). Copyright © 1973, 1978, 1984, 2011 by Biblica, Inc.™. Used by permission. All rights reserved.

Paperback ISBN-13: 978-1-6628-0411-3
Ebook ISBN-13: 978-1-6628-0412-0

Dedication

For anyone I'm able to help while going through their own trials of suffering, depression, mental turmoil—any deep pit of darkness nobody needs to be in. Let's heal together in the spirit of one another with the help of Jesus.

> Heal me, Lord, and I will be healed;
> save me and I will be saved,
> for you are the one I praise.
> Jeremiah 17:14

Contents

Note from author

MY VERY FIRST WRITINGS AS I BEGAN ARE in this book. My struggles with anxiety and emotional struggles are true and at times intense. I have since evolved in my writing, which you'll see as you read through this book. You'll gain a better understanding of how it helped me and I hope it helps in your own healing.

I studied the bible for several years, and later began to take free courses with the Dallas Theological Seminary. During one of those courses, I wrote a very short poem. That is the start of my writing. Not only is gardening therapeutic, writing has also been therapeutic. At times my writing is me telling on paper what and how I feel.

I've tried journaling, but it wasn't any good for me. One day I wrote on just a piece of paper, then found the verse that helped me through this trial of so many emotions I was going through. I felt better putting it on paper along with bible verses. Pretty soon I was writing more, and eventually it all led to this therapeutic book.

If you read pieces that sound repetitive, it means I was still struggling with some emotion, so I kept writing about. I still struggle at times because I am human and have all kinds of feelings, but my happiness is restored.

Sabrina

Ecclesiastes 7:8
The end of a matter is better than its beginning, and patience is better than pride.

My Quiet Time

1 Timothy 2:11
A woman should learn in quietness and full submission.

I DO ENJOY MY QUIET TIME. I CAN FOCUS better on my reading, my studies, and now, I'm happy to say, writing. It feels so good when things flow from my mind, through my pen, and onto paper. My husband told me, "You found your therapy." That is true too. I've said to people, "Reading is my medicine." God does heal.

Holman Illustrated Bible Dictionary say's submission is voluntary placement of oneself under the authority and leadership of another. Leadership of another is me and my husband. It also helps me when there is leadership with another follower that builds their faith—trust and believe God's Words are true. They also have their own quiet time with God alone. They bring the positive I need as the days go by not knowing what each tomorrow will bring.

I have submitted myself in my quiet time to read God's Words every day. His words are food for my soul. I eat up His Words. They are very healing. As I was in the middle of my online theology course, "The story of Scripture," I felt like I was being led somewhere. I didn't know where yet. Several months later I began to write short poems. A few years later I had an accident that made me fall on my head, and it had a big impact on my life, and eventually led to this book today. I continued through those years and still continue to submit and be one on one with God. He has blessed me.

Ephesians 5:21-22
Submit to one another out of reverence for Christ.
Wives, submit yourselves to your own husbands as you do to the Lord.

Depression

Psalm 34:18
The Lord is close to the brokenhearted and saves those
who are crushed in spirit.

Psalm 42:11
Why, my soul, are you downcast? Why so disturbed
within me?
Put your hope in God, for I will yet praise him, my
Savior and my God.

DEPRESSION IS NOT THE SAME AS BEING
sad. Depression goes very deep. I know how it feels.
There's been a lot of times I sit at my desk all day
to do my studies to get me stronger mentally on
God's Words.

Depression is a deep pit that takes a while to get
out of. It could take years or a lifetime to overcome.
A plus for me is how I have an inner circle of people
around me when I need some positive in my life. I
love cats—they are so cuddly when I'm not able
to see or hear my inner circle of people. My cat is

always there for me. Even just to rub her furry belly. She became happy, I became happy.

Look at the positive. Look at what makes you happy. When I get depressed now, I come to think of it as feeling sad with some happy days.

Psalm 3:3
But you, Lord, are a shield around me, my glory, the One who lifts my head high.

Matthew 11:28-30
Come to me, all you who are weary and burdened, and I will give you rest. Take my yoke upon you and learn from me, for I am gentle and humble in heart, and you will find rest for your souls. For my yoke is easy and my burden is light.

Mind Games

1 Peter 5:8
Be alert and of sober mind. Your enemy the devil
prowls around like a roaring lion looking for someone
to devour.

WHEN PEOPLE PLAY WHAT I CALL "MIND games," those people are truly bad. It feels worse when it's someone you've known for almost your whole life. And, Oh My! When you begin to see with your eyes and mind what's been happening, you begin to question the person. Then it begins to turn ugly later, and then becomes even worse!

How do you overcome mind games after you break away from the people who were messing with your mind to bring you down? I'm a fine example of that. I had to seek medical help. I knew I needed more help mentally than what I was reading in the bible. I'm not ashamed of needing medical help. That medical help was needed to heal my stressful self from the ongoing mind games. Everyone has to overcome it in their own way. 1 Peter 5:8 speaks volumes to me—to be watchful and avoid people like that.

Mind games are another kind of emotional hurt that takes time to overcome when there are also other people or family involved in the mind games. They too are affected by them. I was in spiritual warfare. I was battling for several years. This writing is a testimony of my healing in my continued studies and theology courses for even greater healing.

---

1 Timothy 6:4
They are conceited and understand nothing. They have
an unhealthy interest in controversies and quarrels
about words that result in envy, strife, malicious talk,
evil suspicions.

1 Peter 1:13
Therefore, with minds that are alert and fully sober, set
your hope on the grace to be brought to you when
Jesus Christ is revealed at his coming.

My Fear

Isaiah 41:10-13
So do not fear, for I am with you; do not be dismayed,
for I am your God. I will strengthen you and help you;
I will uphold you with my righteous right hand. All
who rage against you will surely be ashamed and dis-
graced; those who oppose you will be as nothing and
perish. Though you search for your enemies, you will
not find them. Those who wage war against you will be
nothing at all. For I am the Lord your God who takes
hold of your right hand and says to you. Do not fear; I
will help you.

FEAR IS A REAL EMOTION THAT PARALYZED
me at home. At my own home! This fear goes back
to the "mind games" I mentioned before. Lies,
harassment, bullying—all these played a part in the
fear that took hold of me.

In my studies, I kept coming to 1 Samuel 22:1-5
and 1 Samuel 24 when David went to hide in the
caves from Saul, and again in 2 Samuel 17 when
David hid in the cave from Absalom. It finally hit

me. I basically did the same thing. I hid in my house to avoid certain people who were very mean. My stomach would get tied up in knots. My insides would begin to shake and then that shaking would work itself to the outside of my body. My heart would beat fast. I had to take my prescriptions to overcome these attacks.

I prayed to God to help them. I even asked God to put His hand on them. Then one day when I was studying I thought, "That's what I need to do." I changed my prayer. I began to pray to God for their salvation. After the third time I prayed to God for their salvation, I began to see small changes. Very slowly I also began to see small changes in myself and started feeling emotionally better.

God knew my heart was in the right place. He still knows my heart.

---

1 Samuel 16:7
But the Lord said to Samuel, "Do not consider his appearance or his height, for I have rejected him. The Lord does not look at the things people look at. People look at the outward appearance, but the Lord looks at the heart."

Psalm 44:21
Would not God have discovered it, since he knows the secrets of the heart?

My Struggles

---

2 Chronicles 16:9
For the eyes of the Lord range throughout the earth
to strengthen those whose hearts are fully com-
mitted to him.

I SOMETIMES GET A CERTAIN FEELING IN
the pit of my stomach. I begin to struggle emotionally and mentally when certain people get close to
me. It's not a good feeling. I know from years of
experience how they're very bad. As I write I collect bible scriptures to help overcome these emotions and anxieties. Why can't these people stay away
from me? I'm beginning to feel like I just want to go
away from here where they can't find me. They have
become my living breathing nightmare.

That has been my struggle. I get to my desk and
begin to read the bible and do my studies to overcome these feelings. And that extra power for me
is now writing to share the words of God through

my trials with scriptures to continue to help me and others.

Joshua 1:5
No one will be able to stand against you all the days of your life. As I was with Moses, so I will be with you; I will never leave you nor forsake you.

Isaiah 40:29
He gives strength to the weary and increases the power of the weak.

1 Corinthians 4:20
For the kingdom of God is not a matter of talk but of power.

Psychological Suffering

Psalm 57:1
Have mercy on me, my God, have mercy on me, for in
you I take refuge. I will take refuge in the shadow of
your wings until the disaster has passed.

PSYCHOLOGICAL SUFFERING IS VERY REAL,
and it is not a good place to be!

Mental anguish and psychological pain was like torture for me. There were people who were causing my mental health to slip at certain points in my life. Now I know what it feels like to rest. I go to my bible and read, read, read, study, study, study, and let me tell you when I do this I feel better. It can take a good while to feel better because my mind was constantly fighting a spiritual battle. I don't like taking the anti-psychotic medicines. They turned me into a zombie. I did nothing but sit, eat, gain weight, and sleep. I like to be active. To avoid those medicines, I've become much more focused on my studies and bible reading. That has become my medicine. It's the positive that helped bring me out of a world of torment.

When you feel yourself slipping into despair, reach for the bible and begin to read! I suggest the Gospel of John to help with healing. Even if you have to read it and reread many times until you begin to feel better. Jesus is your friend and helper.

Matthew 11:28-30
Come to me, all you who are weary and burdened, and I will give you rest. Take my yoke upon you and learn from me, for I am gentle and humble in heart, and you will find rest for your souls. For my yoke is easy and my burden is light.

John 6:27
Do not work for food that spoils, but for food that endures to eternal life, which to Son of Man will give you. For on him God the Father has placed his seal of approval.

Trusting

Matthew 5:10-12
Blessed are those who are persecuted because of righteousness, for theirs is the kingdom of heaven. Blessed
are you when people insult you, persecute you and
falsely say all kinds of evil against you because of me.
Rejoice and be glad, because great is your reward
in heaven, for in the same way they persecuted the
prophets who were before you.

WHEN YOU COME TO THE REALITY OF
losing trust in someone you thought was a true
person, it can be a real heartbreaker. It's another
emotional roller coaster life deals to you.

Life is such a hard pill to swallow at times. Life is
going to continue throwing curve balls at me. I will
learn through some kind of circumstance or through
people who come into my life that will make me
learn something about myself and make me grow
in my faith.

Sometimes life isn't easy. I'll just keep chugging
along with my life. When I come to my eternal life, I

want Jesus to greet me with open arms and a loving hug that says, welcome home.

Romans 8:28
And we know that in all things God works for the good of those who love him, who have been called according to his purpose.

Holy Spirit in Me

1 Corinthians 2:9-16

"What no eye has seen, what no ear has heard, and what no human mind has conceived"—-the things God has prepared for those who love him—-these are the things God has revealed to us by his Spirit. The Spirit searches all things, even the deep things of God. For who knows a person's thoughts except their own spirit within them? In the same way no one knows the thoughts of God except the Spirit of God. What we have received is not the spirit of the world, but the Spirit who is from God, so that we may understand what God has freely given us. This is what we speak, not in words taught us by human wisdom but in words taught by the Spirit, explaining spiritual realities with Spirit-taught words. The person without the Spirit does not accept the things that come from the Spirit of God but considers them foolishness, and cannot understand them because they are discerned only through the Spirit. The person with the Spirit makes judgments about all things, but such a person is not subject to merely human judgments, for "who has known the mind of the Lord so as to instruct him." But we have the mind of Christ.

1 Corinthians 2:9-16 is how I fully understood the Holy Spirit and how the Holy Spirit works in me. The Holy Spirit you cannot see at all. It lives inside me. Not just lives inside me, but also is teaching and guides me. He convicts me when I do wrongs. Then pray for forgiveness. He's giving me his knowledge and thoughts. That is why for me I cannot slack on reading the bible and my studies. I got to keep my Spirit alive so he can guide me, teach me, and help me and to convict me.

John 14:26
But the Advocate, the Holy Spirit, whom the Father will send in my name, will teach you all things and will remind you of everything I have said to you.

Romans 8:26
In the same way, the Spirit helps us in our weakness. We do not know what we ought to pray for, but the Spirit himself intercedes for us through wordless groans.

Titus 3:6
Whom he poured out on us generously through Jesus Christ our Savior.

I'm Reminded of Paul's Thorn

2 Corinthians 12:7-10
Therefore, in order to keep me from becoming conceited, I was given a thorn in my flesh, a messenger of Satan, to torment me. Three times I pleaded with the Lord to take it away from me. But he said to me, "My grace is sufficient for you, for my power is made perfect in weakness." Therefore I will boast all the more gladly about my weaknesses, so that Christ's power may rest on me. That is why for Christ's sake I delight in weaknesses…For when I am weak, then I am strong.

PAUL TALKS OF HIS THORN, AND BECAUSE of it God received even more glory through Paul. Paul rejoiced through his suffering and weakness and disability (Galatians 4:13-16). Paul came to a point where he viewed his weaknesses as assets and not as liabilities.

For years I've been dealing with headaches and migraines. It took a concussion for me to really take off on writing. This concussion has turned out to be a good and positive outcome in the end. It's my healing that has slowed me down to focus on writing in order to share my struggles, trials, and testimonies. I'm excited about this gift that has been happening with me. I'm also ready to see where else it leads me!

---

1 Corinthians 2:13
This is what we speak, not in words taught us by human wisdom but in words taught by the Spirit, explaining spiritual realities with Spirit-taught words.

1 Corinthians 12:7
Now to each one the manifestation of the Spirit is given for the common good.

God's Light is Everywhere

John 1:5
The light shines in the darkness, and the darkness has
not overcome it.

WHEN I'M OUT IN THE BACKYARD ENJOYING
the night sounds, I love looking at my moon garden.
John 1:5 comes to my mind a lot. I see how the
moonlight transforms it. The moon garden is best
seen at night with your eyes, along with the sounds
of the night like insects and toads and birds. These
sounds make it even more awesome to admire. As I
look up to the moon, I'm also reminded of pictures
of Earth I've seen from space. Earth is a beautiful
planet. You see how different it is from space com-
pared to what we see here on Earth.

I'm also still in a process of transformation
through my walk with Christ. I'll admit, some days
it hasn't been easy. I continue to get stronger as the
days go by.

2 Corinthians 3:18
And we all, who with unveiled faces contemplate the Lord's glory, are being transformed into his image with ever—increasing glory, which comes from the Lord, who is in the Spirit.

Romans 12:2
Do not conform to the pattern of this world, but be transformed by the renewing of your mind. Then you will be able to test and approve what God's will is—his good, pleasing and perfect will.

Anger

Ephesians 4:31
Get rid of all bitterness, rage, and anger, brawling and
slander, along with every form of malice.

I'VE LEARNED ANGER IS THE STRONGEST OF
all passions. I realized during one of my studies how
I was in rebellion against God. It was an emotional
baggage I was carrying. When I realized how I was
in rebellion, I began to pray for forgiveness and ask
for God's help to overcome this anger. One night I
wrote a poem about my anger:

<u>Anger</u>
Anger tears me apart.
I need solitude.
I need healing.
Anger is what I have.
Mentally, I'm struggling.
Mentally, I'm hurting.
I need solitude.
I need healing.

Anger shortens a person's life span. Think of what it truly does to you. It raises blood pressure and makes your heart beat faster. In some people their veins begin to bulge. It also takes a while to calm down from anger. Anger eventually leads to a heart attack.

Colossians 3:8
But now you must also rid yourselves of all such things as these: anger, rage, malice, slander, and filthy language from our lips.

Psalm 4:4
Tremble and do not sin; when you are on your beds, search your hearts and be silent.

Lighthouse Keepers

---

2 Samuel 22:29
You, Lord are my lamp; the Lord turns my darkness
into light.

I LOVE TO READ HISTORICAL FICTION about lighthouses and their keepers, as well as non-fiction books about lighthouses.

In my times of trials. I wish I was a lighthouse keeper from an earlier era for the solitude of it.

A lighthouse keeper's job is far more than just tending to the light. They also keep logs of the tides, weather, ships, or just everyday doings at the lighthouse. They help when ships are in distress. Lighthouse keepers have gone out in dangerous storms to rescue people. They are very courageous. They shelter people who come to the lighthouse for a safe haven when they know a very strong storm is approaching. The lighthouse is the safest place to seek shelter and withstand bad weather.

Another trial the keeper goes through is grief when death is involved from a storm. At times, storms make it difficult to travel across the water. There have been plenty of people saved from the storms thanks to the keeper of the light.

Psalm 43:3
Send me your light and your faithful care, let them lead me.

Matthew 5:14-16
You are the light of the world. A town built on a hill cannot be hidden. Neither do people light a lamp and put it under a bowl. Instead they put it on its stand, and it gives light to everyone in the house. In the same way let your light shine before others, that they may see your good deeds and glorify your Father in heaven.

Loneliness

Psalm 25:16
Turn to me and be gracious to me, for I am lonely and afflicted.

THERE HAVE BEEN A LOT OF TIMES WHEN I feel like I'm alone. When you've helped people, your good ends up being tarnished because other people come into their lives. You begin to feel used. At times people will even lie to try and tarnish your image. Then you begin to feel like you're alone and think to yourself, "I don't deserve that."

The world is huge and has billions of people. You would never think that when loneliness sets in. It's not a happy feeling.

I've heard several people say, "I love him or her, but I don't like them." If I get the feeling someone doesn't like me. I do what I can to leave that person alone. I'm not going to push myself onto that person. After I say "Hi" and that person looks away, or you ask a question and it goes unanswered, it's another kind of lonely feeling—the kind you get when you're ignored.

I have a sticky note on my desk with a quote written on it that I read somewhere. I don't remember where I read it or who said it. I catch myself reading it sometimes. "Comfort my lonely soul and still my trembling heart." For someone to say that means I'm not the only one who feels lonely.

---

1 Samuel 12:22
For the sake of his great name the Lord will not reject his people, because the Lord was pleased to make you his own.

Psalm 147:3
He heals the brokenhearted and binds up their wounds.

My Help on God's Timing

Habakkuk 2:3
For the revelation awaits an appointed time; it speaks of
the end and will not prove false. Though it linger, wait
for it; it will certainly come and will not delay.

IN MY STUDIES, I WAS WANTING TO LEARN
more about God's timing. As I read the bible, I
learned His timing can be very long, even decades,
or as quick as just one month.

Nadab, a King of Israel, reigned for two years (1
Kings 15:25-30), Ahab became king of Israel and
reigned in Samaria for twenty-two years (1Kings
16:29-33), Menahem was a king of Israel who
reigned for ten years (2 Kings 15:17-20), and Hoshea
the last king of Israel who reigned for nine years (2
Kings 17:1-6). Manasseh was a king of Judah who
reigned for fifty-five years (2 Chronicles 33:1-6).

I use these kings as an example of the years they
reigned and did evil in the eyes of the Lord. This
helped me understand some of God's timing and

how we need to persevere through trials. God's timing takes patience. It might take years of keeping my peace and patience along with testing me while I wait for God's reward.

Ecclesiates 3:11
He had made everything beautiful in its time. He has also set eternity in the human heart; yet no one can fathom what God has done from beginning to end.

2 Peter 3:8-9
But do not forget this one thing, dear friends: With the Lord a day is like a thousand years, and a thousand years are like a day. The Lord is not slow in keeping his promise, as some understand slowness. Instead he is patient with you, not wanting anyone to perish, but everyone to come to repentance.

How to Overcome Betrayal

Luke 21:15-19
For I will give you words and wisdom that none of
your adversaries will be able to resist or contradict. You
will be betrayed even by parents, brothers and sisters,
relatives and friends, and they will put some of you to
death. Everyone will hate you because of me. But not
a hair on your head will perish. Stand firm, and you
will win life.

THIS IS STILL TRUE TODAY. AS I BEGAN TO
read the bible every day and got deeper in my studies,
I tuned in more to how people can change. When
they began to cause trouble with me and my family,
I had to let them go. That was hard because in some
cases they were people I've known for many years.

After the initial shock from the people I trusted,
I had to overcome it emotionally, and then later on
(however long it took me) I had to come to the
reality of what's done is done. Nobody can change
the history of betrayal.

Everyone that's been betrayed has been saved by the ultimate betrayal. Judas betrayed Jesus (Luke 22-23). Betrayal is part of God's plan. My road to healing began when I realized this powerful idea.

John 16:33
"I have told you these things, so that in me you may have peace. In this world you will have trouble. But take heart! I have overcome the world."

1 John 5:4
For everyone born of God overcomes the world. This is the victory that has overcome the world, even our faith.

Positive Influence

Proverbs 13:20
Walk with the wise and become wise, for a companion
of fools suffers harm.

DOLLY PARTON AND REBA MCENTIRE ARE
two famous celebrities who are inspiring to me. They
are positive people. I think of my trials and suffering, but then I see them and begin to remember
they've talked about how their faith has helped them.
They've persevered.

Everyone needs positive people in their life. I've
learned I do. People who complain a lot about tiny
things—it's too negative. Tiny things will grow into
something bigger that can be depressing to hear.

When It comes to other people who also inspire
me from television or reading their books, I think of
Charles Stanley, Stormie Omartian, and Joyce Meyer.
I recently read a book Charlie Daniels wrote about
his life lessons and wisdom he learned along the way.
They all talk about what they have gone through in

the past and how they overcame those things. Now they've reached out to help lots of other people. They are encouraging me to do the same.

Proverbs 1:5
Let the wise listen and add to their learning, and let the discerning get guidance.

Proverbs 1:7
The fear of the Lord is the beginning of knowledge, but fools despise wisdom and instruction.

Proverbs 12:15
The way of fools seems right to them, but the wise listen to advice.

From Darkness to Light

---

1 Peter 2:9
You are a chosen people...God's special possession, that
you may declare the praises of him who called you out
of darkness into his wonderful light.

I DON'T KNOW ANY MORE HOW TO TELL
who a true person is. I thought I had true people in
my life, but for so many years now it seems everyone
has turned on me. It is like my world continually falls
apart. I get sad at times wondering and waiting to
see if the few people who are still with me are going
to turn against me as well.

God wants us to trust Him. Faith is a lifelong
process. When those thoughts come to my mind,
I'm on the verge of darkness. I pull myself back into
the light and read His Words.

Isaiah 55:8-9
For my thoughts are not your thoughts, neither are your ways my ways...As the heavens are higher than the earth, so are my ways higher than your ways and my thoughts than your thoughts."

John 14:20
...I am in my Father, and you are in me, and I am in you.

Colossians 2:6-7
Just as you received Christ Jesus as Lord, continue to live your lives in him, rooted and built up in him, strengthened in the faith as you were taught, and over-flowing with thankfulness.

Answered Prayer from Strongholds

2 Corinthians 10:4
The weapons we fight with are not the weapons of
the world. On the contrary, they have divine power to
demolish strongholds.

THE KEY WORD FOR ME IS *DIVINE* (FROM
God) added to *power*. This makes for a very strong
verse in the bible along with many more. I was in a
stronghold for five years. I persevered and stood my
ground, along with the suffering from this stronghold. God answered my prayers.

That was the hardest five years of my life. This
is why you need people you are influenced by who
inspire you to keep going forward. Do not give up!
I kept reading and studying the bible to remind
myself God is with me. At times it felt like my world
was falling in around me. I've had a tremendous
learning experience about people throughout this
whole ordeal as everything kept coming at me day
after day after day.

Each one of us will have some kind of stronghold that is very difficult in life. It's very important to keep praying and reading the bible until it has passed. Thank God for answered prayers! When He answers your prayer, don't stop with your prayer time or your bible reading. Keep building stronger trust and faith in knowing God is working on your behalf to continue to be a conqueror.

Psalm 34:4,17

I sought the Lord, and he answered me; he delivered me from all my fears. The righteous cry out, and the Lord hears them; he delivers them from all their troubles.

1 John 4:4

You, dear children, are from God and have overcome them, because the one who is in you is greater than the one who is in the world.

West Texas

Deuteronomy 32:10
In a desert land he found him, in a barren and howling
waste. He shielded him and cared for him; he guarded
him as the apple of his eye.

Isaiah 35:1,6
The desert and the parched land will be glad; the wilderness will rejoice and blossom...Water will gush forth
in the wilderness and streams in the desert.

AS WE TRAVEL DOWN FREEWAYS OR
country roads there is so much natural beauty like
wildflowers, grasses, rocks, and cliffs. I love the
enjoyment of looking at all those natural landscapes.

West Texas has become my favorite place to go.
Lots of vast openness to admire. West Texas has
deserts, mountains, canyons, lakes, and one of the
largest rivers running through it. The animals that
live in the Chihuahuan Desert along with reptiles,
insects, birds, and amphibians know how to sur-
vive. The Rio Grande runs through the Chihuahuan

Desert—there's some natural water for all with the Rio Grande.

What man created are the windmills. I also enjoy looking at them. Windmills serve a purpose by pumping natural water from the ground. A few times, I've seen cows drinking the water the windmills provide. Not just cows but the wild animals come to drink the water too. I love the invention of the windmills, it's just so old timey to me. In the desert, God has provided for their needs of survival with food and water, even if one is created by people to pump natural water from the ground to drink throughout West Texas.

We go through stages of loneliness, confusion, discouragement, and I have to add psychological troubles. This is our wilderness. Jesus was led into the desert (his wilderness is described in Matthew 4:1-11). God was preparing Jesus for a new beginning in his ministry. Jesus passed his trials. His love for us kept him going. He knew God was there through his whole time in the wilderness. God is always at work in our lives. God teaches us through our suffering and tribulations to dependend on Him and His plan for our life.

Even when we are the ones who feel so isolated and alone in the desert to fend for our own self, God does provide for our needs to persevere in our wilderness. We too can pass our trials with the help of God, just like Jesus did.

Isaiah 43: 19-20

I am doing a new thing! Now it springs up; do you not perceive it? I am making a way in the wilderness and streams in the wasteland...Because I provide water in the wilderness and streams in the wasteland, to give drink to my people, my chosen.

Luke 4:1

Jesus, full of the Holy Spirit, left Jordan and was led by the Spirit into the wilderness.

One Small Action

Zephaniah 3:17
The Lord your God is with you, the Mighty Warrior
who saves. He will take great delight in you; in his love
he will no longer rebuke you, but will rejoice over you
with singing.

I SPRAY PERFUME ON ME. IT WAS AN ACT towards the positive. The smell is already making me feel better. An act that seems so small can lead to something much bigger in my mental state. I tell my husband, son, and his fiancé I love them. Hearing them say "I love you too" does a positive thing to my mental state. When I get out of my slumps and do some cleaning, that also does wonders to my mental state. I've accomplished something today.

Even when depression rears its ugly head again, I know my Mighty Warrior is with me. He delights in how I can overcome by doing small things to help it pass. I'm back in my bible reading and studies, and now writing after several years have passed without taking anti-psychotic medicine. My nerves healed. I knew I needed to get off those drugs. Nowadays, depression isn't an ongoing day-to-day ordeal. He's rejoicing over me (and you) with singing because we took the initiative to do some small acts on the road to healing and recovery.

Psalm 55:22
Cast your cares on the Lord and he will sustain you; he will never let the righteous be shaken.

Luke 12:3
What you have said in the dark will be heard in the daylight, and what you have whispered in the ear in the inner rooms will be proclaimed from roofs

---

Sadness

Psalm 34:17-19
The righteous cry out, and the Lord hears them; he
delivers them from all their troubles. The Lord is close
to the brokenhearted and saves those who are crushed
in spirit. The righteous person may have many troubles,
but the Lord delivers him from them all.

Sadness about how it seems I've failed
at part of my life can feel like I'm mourning because
I don't know how to go about overcoming what I
feel I've failed in. I feel lost. But I have to keep on
keeping on with each day. It seems so hard because
my sadness is deep.

I've come to a point of wondering why a lot of
my prayers just seem to go in the opposite direction.
Sometimes I have zero understanding of what's happening or why. All I've been able to do is praise Jesus
and praise God until my sadness, depression, or this
deeper kind of hurt passes. Some were situations
that never should have happened and yet they did,

and I'm still trying to come to grips with. It's taking a while to forget, and maybe I will never forget. So I keep praising the most Holy One who has the power of the eternal world in his hand. I know one day things will get better. It's just a matter of when.

We all go through emotional difficulties throughout our lifetime. It's very hard at times. I go to my quiet place to be alone with God.

Psalm 38:9
All my longings lie open before you, Lord; my sighing is not hidden for you.

Ecclesiastes 1:18
For with much wisdom comes much sorrow; the more knowledge, the more grief.

Matthew 5:4
Blessed are those who mourn, for they will be comforted.

When People Have Already Judged You

John 15:20
Remember what I told you: "A servant is not greater than his master. If they persecuted me, they will persecute you also. If they obeyed my teaching, they will obey yours also."

JOHN 15:20 SAYS IT ALL FOR ME. PEOPLE are very persuasive and smooth talkers when it comes to letting other people judging other people just by their smooth-talking, easy-to-believe way of how they speak.

This all goes back to the serpent and Eve (Genesis 3). You read how easily the serpent changed Eve's mind to eat the apple. Then Eve gave Adam the apple to eat also (Genesis 3:6). The cycle of smooth-talking judgement of other people does affect how people view things, to the point of believing the lies that are told, like the serpent did to Eve.

The Old Testament is just as important as the New Testament. Read and understand the Old Testament better. You'll see the importance of Jesus and have a better understanding why Jesus needed to come.

Later on (it could take years), people will see how they have wrongly judged a person just by all the smooth talking and deceitfulness. One day that person will come out as they really are. One day I'll go to my real home. We who believe are all citizens in the Kingdom of God. Jesus is preparing my home (John 14:1-2). There will be no lies, judgement, or hate in the kingdom of God.

Psalm 62:4
Surely they intend to topple me from my lofty place; they take delight in lies. With their mouths they bless, but in their hearts they curse.

John 5:22-23
Moreover, the Father judges no one, but has entrusted all judgement to the Son, that all may honor the Son just as they honor the Father. Whoever does not honor the Son does not honor the Father, who sent him

Acts 10:42-43
He commanded us to preach to the people and to testify that he is one whom God appointed as judge of the living and the dead. All the prophets testify about him that everyone who believes in him receives forgiveness of sins through his name.

Visualization

Philippians 4:8-9
...If anything is excellent or praiseworthy—think about
such things. Whatever you have learned or received
or heard from me, or seen in me—put it into practice.
And the God of peace will be with you.

IN MY STUDIES I LIKE TO VISUALIZE. I
looked up the priest garments (Exodus 28), for
example. That's a description with a lot of details
about the garment. It is a very pretty garment. That
is part of my knowledge on learning in my studies
and I absorb it better in my brain to retain it. Later I
will use this in my writings. I get so much enjoyment
from my studies, and I learn a great deal.

Right now as I was writing I got a weird feeling
happening in my head. I'm still healing from the
concussion. My therapist said the weirdness in my
head is my blood moving. I like my therapist. She is a
God-fearing lady, she brought me positivity and was
always happy. I'm not feeling well right now, since I

can't read for long or take a theology course online at the moment. I have my pad and pen, though, and write what comes to my mind. I'm persevering through this suffering with my head to continue with what helps me feel better. My mind is on what I've already learned and retained. God's Words are the true medicine that is taking my mind off of some of this weirdness and the hurt that is happening.

The vision of Jesus on the cross and his suffering comes to my mind often. My headaches and all the other happenings with my head are temporary.

---

2 Corinthians 1:5-6
For just as we share abundantly in the sufferings of Christ, so also our comfort abounds through Christ. If we are distressed, it is for your comfort and salvation; if we are comforted, it is for your comfort, which produces in you patient endurance of the same sufferings we suffer.

Psalm 119:50
My comfort in my suffering is this: Your promise preserves my life.

Warning Flags

Exodus 17:15
Moses built an altar and called it The Lord is
my banner.

SOMEONE CAME TO OUR DOOR. MY SON
came and got me because he didn't feel comfortable
answering. I looked out the peephole and didn't see
anyone. The guy my son saw was wearing a baseball
cap with half his face showing. The eyes and nose
were hiding. My son's warning flag was raised to red.

All the beaches along the U.S. have warning flags.
I've only been to the Texas Gulf Coast. One of the
popular beaches for vacationers has colored warning
flag: Green means conditions are calm; yellow means
caution when entering the water; red means strong
winds, strong surf, and strong current; and purple's
an indicator of potential problems with jellyfishes.

My son had a strong inner knowing. He walked
away from the door. The Holy Spirit in him gave
him a warning that raised a red flag for him. I shop

a lot on Amazon. There have been many times I've cancelled orders. My inner knowing was telling me I'll be in trouble. The Holy Spirit gave me a warning that raised the yellow flag.

The Holy Spirit works in your inner self. Your inner self is your conscience. Your conscience tells you when something is not right. We listened to our conscience and what the Holy Spirit was telling us.

In the book of Acts (Acts 16:6-10), Paul listened to the Holy Spirit. The Holy Spirit did not permit them to enter.

Acts 16:6-7

Paul and his companions traveled throughout the region of Phrygia and Galatia, having been kept by the Holy Spirit from preaching the words in the province of Asia. When they came to the border of Mysia, they tried to enter Bithynia, but the Spirit of Jesus would not allow them to.

Seasons of Change

Ecclesiastes 3:1-8
There is a time for everything, and a season for every
activity under the heavens...

LOOK AT HOW THE SEASONS CHANGE.
Summer brings shade trees that provide relief from
the sun. Fall brings the beauty of colors in the trees,
plus it brings a cooling down. Winter brings the
beauty of snow and bare branches on trees. Spring
brings the beauty of new growth in trees and flowers
begin to bloom, plus it brings the rain.

God is the author of days. God is omnipresent.
He is in every moment of my everyday life. Our seasons of life are birth, childhood, adolescence, adult-
hood, old age, and death. Throughout our seasons,
our culture and social activities change as well. Life
changes rapidly or easily, at times emotionally.

God calls us to change, and by our spirit to
change. The change is a privilege. It is the nature
of God to work in the midst of change for Spiritual

fruit to appear. We must be planted in the Word of God. As we face adversity, affliction, and discipline, our lives and the fruit begin to change and appear. It takes time and often requires tremendous patience—it doesn't happen overnight.

With God in our lives we are changed into a more meaningful person, with the experience and wisdom that will continue to guide us as we walk through our changing seasons.

James 1:17-18

Every good and perfect gift is from above, coming down from the Father of the heavenly lights, who does not change like shifting shadows. He chose to give us birth through the word of truth, that we might be a kind of firstfruits of all created.

1 John 2:24-25

As for you, see that what you have heard from the beginning remains in you. If it does, you also will remain in the Son and in the Father. And this is what he promised us—-eternal life.

Rest

Genesis 2:2
By the seventh day God had finished the work he had
been doing; so on the seventh day he rested from
all his work.

EVERYONE NEEDS REST AND A GOOD
night's sleep. You are at ease when you rest. It does
wonders for your spirit to continue with everyday life.

I was just reading about an influential person
who fell ill from exhaustion and died. This person
lived to be eighty years old. I'm over fifty years old
now. I know I've slowed down. There are times your
body will let you know you need rest. Listen to what
your body tells you. Your body knows your limits.

Rest reduces stress. Rest boosts your immune
system. Rest restores mental energy and creativity.
Creativity helps me in writing about my own life
experiences I can use as examples for helping others.

I took his yoke, my relationship is established
(Matthew 11: 28-30). Psalm 23 is a calming Psalm

to say before sleep. When I say it, I visualize myself in that place.

Jeremiah 31: 25
I will refresh the weary and satisfy the faint.

Psalm 4:8
In peace I will lie down and sleep, for you alone, Lord, make me dwell in safety.

Mark 6:31
Then, because so many people were coming and going that they did not even have a chance to eat, he said to them, "Come with me by yourselves to a quiet place and get some rest."

Loyalty

Deuteronomy 7:9
Know therefore that the Lord your God is God; he
is the faithful God, keeping his covenant of love to a
thousand generations of those who love him and keep
his commandments.

LOYALTY IS ABOUT BEING SUPPORTIVE AND
maintaining your allegiance. That is how God is, but
He is much more than just loyal. If you think about
it, loyalty is an important word. You will see the
people who come into your life and the people who
will leave your life, the people who continue to stay
in your life when you go through one trial, then it
seems you have another trial. The people who have
stayed through all your trials have stayed loyal to
you. They supported you, they helped in healing you
from the times you felt broken.

Just think how you feel knowing the loyalty of
the people who have stayed loyal to you. God is your
supernatural power of loyalty, love, and faithfulness.

God goes above and beyond for His children who are here on earth with answered prayers and the many blessings He has given. We have so much to be thankful for, so let God know by thanking Him in your private time with Him, in the name of Jesus.

Proverbs 3:1-2
My son, do not forget my teaching, but keep my commands in your heart, for they will prolong your life many years and bring you peace and prosperity.

Lamentations 3:22-24
Because of the Lord's great love we are not consumed, for his compassions never fail. They are new every morning; great is your faithfulness. I say to myself, "The Lord is my portions; therefore I will wait for him.

How I see the Heart

Psalm 41:9
Even my close friend, someone I trusted, one who
shared my bread, has turned against me.

PSALM 41 IS A PRAYER FOR HELP AGAINST
betrayal. David's friend Ahithophel (2 Samuel 16:20;
17:1-4, 23) became disloyal and deceitful—a real
backstabber. Ahithophel ran when his advice failed
and then hung himself. He didn't want to face David
or how he betrayed him.

You think you know people from years of friendship. Like David, we were blind because they seemed
to be genuine. I began to ask myself, "How can I
know who a true friend or person is when I meet
them?" I have no one I can call my friend anymore.
For me now, I look at the heart of people even more.
You see the heart through their eyes.

The eyes are a reflection of the heart. When
someone talks but doesn't want to look at your
eyes, it tells me they are hiding something they don't

want to reveal. Their eyes will also reveal if they are friendly or not friendly. I do want to make clear here how there is a difference between someone who is shy and someone who is hiding, or someone like me who has a head injury where they have to look away to focus on the first word to make a sentence. When you become a follower of Christ and study God's Words in the bible, your own eyes and ears help in seeing people's hearts. Your brain (mind) will be able to process someone's eyes.

Romans 1:21
For although they knew God, they neither glorified him as God nor gave thanks to him, but their thinking became futile and their foolish hearts were darkened.

My Own Helpful Therapy

Proverbs 4:20-22
My son, pay attention to what I say; turn your ear to
my words. Do not let them out of your sight, keep
them within your heart; for they are life to those who
find them and health to one's whole body.

I READ A LOT PLUS STUDY A LOT, AND NOW
add in writing. All three are my therapy. I don't
need medication when I do these, and they are very
helpful for my mind and spirit.

I saw the words sunshine and shadow. Sunshine
means cheerfulness and happiness. Shadow means
gloom or that which causes gloom (gloom means
darkness or sadness). Mindful meditation is helping
me to focus, visualize, and meditate on God's Word
to heal emotionally, mentally, and spiritually.

Don't let the shadow of suffering or persecution
keep you in the shadow. Persevere towards the sunshine for the beautiful reward of the healing heart
the sunshine brings. Your own testimony will help

others with our own personal wisdom that comes out of the shadow of gloom.

Jeremiah 17:14
Heal me, Lord, and I will be healed; save me and I will be saved for you are the one I praise.

Jeremiah 33:6
I will bring health and healing to it; I will heal my people and will let them enjoy abundant peace and security.

1 Peter 2:24
He himself bore our sins in his body on the cross, so that we might die to sins and live for righteousness, by his wounds you have been healed.

Guardian Angels

Psalm 91:11
For he will command his angels concerning you to
guard you in all your ways.

HAVE YOU EVER HEARD SOMEONE SAY, "MY guardian angel was looking out for me" or "My guardian angel saved me?" There is truth in that. God uses His heavenly angels in many ways.

Just think back to those times in your life where you thought you should have died. I do have one incident that happened to me when I was eighteen or nineteen years old where I could have died. My time on earth wasn't ready to end.

Jesus said, "For I tell you that their angels in heaven always see the face of my Father in heaven" (Matthew 18:10). Angels are in constant communication with God. It is through God the angels work—the where, when, and how are all on God's orders. It is very important to know and remember all power flows from God. Angels are God's servants.

Our ultimate guardian is God. He's ruler over all the angels. Thank God for His heavenly protection through His angels as we live each day not knowing what tomorrow will bring. Isn't that a wonderful feeling to have? That is one way God protects you in the spiritual realm.

Psalm 34:6-7
This poor man called, and the Lord heard him; he saved him out of all his troubles. The angel of the Lord encamps around those who fear him, and he delivers them.

Colossians 1:16
For in him all things were created: things in heaven and on earth, visible and invisible, whether thrones or powers or rulers or authorities; all things have been created through him and for him.

Hebrews 1:14
Are not all angels ministering spirits sent to serve those who will inherit salvation?

My Life Changed

Matthew 4:19-20
"Come, follow me," Jesus said, "and I will send you out to fish for people." At once they left their nets and followed him.

GROWING UP WE WENT TO CHURCH AND Sunday school when I spent summers with my granny and grandad. We went every Sunday and Wednesday. Then I went to work and left home. I started life away from home and didn't think of church or Sunday school anymore. I didn't even read the bible. Many years later, I realized how badly I slacked off and lost the importance of God's Words to help guide me through life and with the right people. I truly paid the price for being a slacker!

Spiritually, I was only praying when I felt like I had to. I only read Scriptures perhaps once a year. I had the good common sense to know right from wrong. Because of this common sense, I learned of the wrongs I kept hearing (this too goes back to mind games). This brought me back to reading and studying the bible to help me spiritually persevere through these trials, along with lots of prayers for His help.

John 3:3
Jesus replied, "very truly I tell you, no one can see the kingdom of God unless they are born again."

Ephesians 5:15-16
Be very careful, then how you live—not as unwise but as wise, making the most of every opportunity, because the days are evil.

1 Peter 1:3
Praise be to the God and Father of our Lord Jesus Christ! In his great mercy he has given us new birth into a living hope through the resurrection of Jesus Christ from the dead.

The Woods

Hebrews 8:2
Who serves in the sanctuary, the true tabernacle set up
by the Lord, not by a mere human being.

MY MEMORIES TAKE ME TO MY GRANNY
and grandad's place. They lived in the middle of
the woods. It was so pleasant and peaceful, especially in the morning when dew was on everything.
It smelled so good. The pine trees would sway when
the wind blew. Underneath, the pine needles gath-
ered on the ground, and wild blackberry vines grew.
It was such a treat to just pluck a blackberry off its
vine and eat it. We'd see deer. At one point we saw
a fawn. Snakes would wander close to the house and
lots of daddy long leg spiders. That's a spider I hav-
en't seen in many years.

Just think of your own sanctuary where you have
nature, your own safe place, your own refuge, your
own quiet place. It's someplace where you can just
find calmness in yourself, when you need alone time.

Psalm 46:1
God is our refuge and strength, an ever-present help
in trouble.

Psalm 143:5
I remember the days of long ago; I meditate on all your
works and consider what your hands have done.

Circumcision of the Heart

Romans 2:28-29
A person is not a Jew who is one only outwardly, nor
is circumcision merely outward and physical. No, a
person is a Jew who is one inwardly; and circumcision
is circumcision of the heart, by the Spirit, not by the
written code. Such a person's praise is not from other
people, but from God.

MY UNDERSTANDING OF CIRCUMCISION IS
to cut away the flesh. In asking God to sanctify and
circumcise your ear, you're asking Him to make your
ears sensitive to hear what is Holy and right. To
remove worldly temptations, circumcision of the
heart is removing that outer hardness you've built
around your heart. Circumcision of the heart is
spiritual, and it's what brings out kindness, humility,
faith, hope, and love.

I'm pretty deep in my studies and love it. Because
I haven't read the bible steadily for many years, my
upbringing from childhood has kept me grounded.
It's people who entered my life and at times made

me harden my heart. I've been truly hurt. My bible reading and studies have removed this hardness around my heart, which I put there myself. I blame myself because I thought nothing could or would happen—the people seemed to be true people but weren't. I'm glad this kind of drama all took less than ten years. I see James 1:22-25 differently because I lived through the people who are one way and then became someone different. Now I listen carefully to people and what they are really saying. I'm very observant of their words. My heart is open. I'm on guard!

Deuteronomy 10:16
Circumcise your hearts, therefore, and do not be stiff-necked any longer.

Psalm 73:26
My flesh and my heart may fail, but God is the strength of my heart and my portion forever.

You've Been Lassoed

2 Peter 3:18
But grow in the grace and knowledge of our Lord and Savior Jesus Christ. To him be glory both now and forever! Amen.

A LASSO IS USED TO CATCH CATTLE AND horses. The lasso is a rope that tightens around the neck (with care).

Here's an example you can visualize. You've lassoed your troubles and problems very close to you. That lasso is wrapped around your heart and is causing bitterness, anger, and unforgiveness. As you grow with Christ, the anger, bitterness, and unforgiveness slowly loosen. As it loosens you're allowing God into that area to work with you. When that little area that has loosened it has experienced healing, then you loosen the lasso a little more. God again enters where you loosened the lasso and begins more healing. The more you loosen up the lasso that was wrapped around your heart. You will begin to see how God is working in you and for you on your behalf. This was my heart at work towards my healing. You'll feel great over time because you begin to feel the Spiritual love, knowing God has had your back all along (Jeremiah 33:3).

When it comes to matters of the heart our Spiritual growth is a lifelong process. Pray continuously (1 Thessalonians 5:17) so that when your heart becomes compromised your feelings won't fester into deeper emotions.

Luke 18:1

Then Jesus told his disciples a parable to show them that they should always pray and not give up.

No Favoritism

Acts 10:34-35

Then Peter began to speak: "I now realize how true it
is that God does not show favoritism but accepts from
every nation the one who fears him and does what
is right."

PRAY FOR YOUR BULLIES. PRAY FOR THE
people who have done you wrong. Like Saul (Acts
9). They can be turned around to be God-fearing,
kinder worshippers of God and spread the gospel.

God loves every single person here on this planet.
We as humans tend to be influenced by people. Some
people are not the right ones to be influenced by as 1
Corinthians 15:33 says, do not be misled: "Bad com-
pany corrupts good character." Some people like all
kinds of drama in their lives, and let me tell you, if
you let them in your life there will be no peace.

Take something as small as visiting someone's
house, for example. They see a penny somewhere
on the floor beside the couch, and they take it. That

penny adds up to more cents this person they are visiting could use to buy a loaf of bread. With one less penny, it's going to take time to get that penny back that was taken.

One cent to some people might not seem so important. But to a lot of people one cent is very important. Think of the small things that truly matter in people's lives. Saul persecuted the church, dragging men and women to prison after Stephen was stoned to death (Acts 8: 1-3). In Acts 9 his life turned around when Jesus spoke to him. God shows no favoritism. Jesus still comes into our lives today.

---

1 Corinthians 10:13
No temptation has overtaken you except what is common to mankind. And God is faithful; he will not let you be tempted beyond what you can bear. But when you are tempted, he will also provide a way out so that you can endure it.

Be the Shepherd

Acts 20:28-32

Keep watch over yourselves and all the flock of which
the Holy Spirit has made you overseers. Be shepherds
of the church of God, which he bought with his own
blood. I know that after I leave, savage wolves will
come in among you and will not spare the flock. Even
from your own number men will arise and distort the
truth in order to draw away disciples after them. So be
on your guard! Remember that for three years I never
stopped warning each of you night and day with tears.
Now I commit you to God and to the word of his
grace, which can build you up and give you an inheritance among all those who are sanctified.

THINK OF PAUL AS THE SHEPHERD. HE CON-
tinued speaking the truth of God's words and the
reason for Jesus to come and save us. Not only is
Jesus our shepherd, He is our light in this world
filled with darkness because of sin. There are people
out there in this world like Paul who keep the savage
wolves away from us, who want to keep us seeing the

light, to keep reaching out to God for His guidance in your life. Keep that light shining and be a shepherd also, in the name of Jesus.

John 8:12

When Jesus spoke again to the people, he said, "I am the light of the world. Whoever follows me will never walk in darkness, but will have the light of life."

John 12:46-47

I have come into the world as a light, so that no one who believes in me should stay in darkness. If anyone hears my words but does not keep them, I do not judge that person. For I did not come to judge the world, but to save the world.

Different Garments

John 11:43-44
When he had said this, Jesus called in a loud voice,
"Lazarus, come out!"

JESUS KNEW WHEN LAZARUS CAME OUT, HE
wanted Lazarus in new proper clothes and out of the
burial clothes.

Look at the different types of garments: burial
garments, garments for weddings, garments for
interviews, garments for summer wear, garments for
winter wear. There are many choices for choosing
what to wear for outer wear from everyday routines
to some type of special event.

Look at the spiritual change in yourself. It's how
people see you as a person. It is not all about how
you dress and present yourself in nice clothes and
jewelry that match. The spiritual change is in the
heart that beats inside of you.

1 Peter 3:2-5

When they see the purity and reverence of your lives. Your beauty should not come from outward adornment, such as elaborate hairstyles and the wearing of gold jewelry of fine clothes. Rather, it should be that of your inner self, the unfading beauty of gentle and quiet spirit which is of great worth in God's sight. For this is the way the holy women of the past who put their hope in God used to adorn themselves.

Peace

John 14:27
Peace I leave with you; my peace I give you. I do not
give to you as the world gives. Do not let your hearts
be troubled and do not be afraid.

WHILE I WAS STUDYING ONE DAY, I FELT
like I was on a real soft cushion and wrapped up in
invisible wings. That is the best description I can give.
I loved that feeling. John 14:27 came to my mind
as I sank into peace feeling wrapped up in unseen
love. It was just a wonderful feeling. Twice this has
happened to me, and I have never felt anything like
it. I won't forget that kind of enveloping comfort.

The Holy Spirit is flowing in the Spirit with
love-producing power. This love comes from faith.
It is faith in God's Word. We trust and rest in it when
we read God's promises and meditate on His Word.
He keeps Himself quietly beneath the surface for
us to drink when we are thirsty. He will glorify you.

Psalm 91:4
He will cover you with his feathers, and under his wings you will find refuge; his faithfulness will be your shield and rampart.

Ending Friendships

Proverbs 13:20
Walk with the wise and become wise, for a companion
of fools suffers harm.

THIS VERSE WOKE ME UP ALONG WITH
what I kept hearing. If I hadn't opened my eyes and
ears to what I kept hearing, I would to this day keep
lowering myself to the level of the person who was
causing strife with me, my family, and my marriage.
Another friendship had to come to an end. Almost
two years later, I had to text this person about the
stuff that was still at our house. The response I got
back upset me! The fools like in Proverbs 13:20
don't like ending things gracefully. The distancing
of myself from fools makes life much more pleasant.
There were times I felt upset. During those times, I
would come to my desk to do what I'm now calling
my therapy. Psalm 37:3 says, "Trust in the Lord
and do good; dwell in the land and enjoy safe pas-
ture." David called for trust despite the presence

of evil men because they will wither in the grass (Psalm 37:2).

It's an emotional process we go through when you see the true person come out. Even after years of a friendship you've seen a whole other side you want no part of. You'll become a stronger person by letting that person go. Your gut knew and you listened to it—not just your gut but your heart as well. I want to share friendships through writing. Here is a lovely verse I'll leave you with:

Proverbs 27:9
Perfume and incense bring joy to the heart, and the pleasantness of a friend springs from their heartfelt advice.

Weak Versus Strong

Acts 4:13
When they saw the courage of Peter and John and realized that they were unschooled, ordinary men, they were astonished and they took note that these men had been with Jesus

PETER AND JOHN WERE CALLED. WE CAN also spend time with Jesus and his words. The bible is available 24/7/365. Your own knowledge comes from your own life experience and how you choose to share. I can't afford a higher education. I've invested in books along with several bibles and bible study tools with the free online courses with the Dallas Theological Seminary.

People made me to be a person with a lot of mental problems because I would continue to defend myself against bullies who would twist stuff about me and my family because they thought I was weak. That goes back to mind games. My mind is strong, my eyes are strong, my ears are strong. Jesus sees who I am. When God is ready for me to come home, my book will continue to help and heal other people.

---

1 Corinthians 1:26-28

Think of what you were when you were called. Not many of you were wise by human standards; not many were influential; not many were of noble birth. But God chose the foolish things of the world to shame the wise; God chose the weak things of the world to shame the strong. God chose the lowly things of this world and despised things—and the things that are not—to nullify the things that are.

Our Mortal Body

Micah 6:8
He has shown you O mortal, what is good. And what
does the Lord require of you? To act justly and to love
mercy and to walk humbly with your God.

WE ARE MORTAL, FLESH AND BONES THAT
decay after we die. God wants us to obey Him, but
not out of some obligation. When we obey we do
it inwardly. We feel His presence in us. Out of obligation, it is "I'll do what I feel like." That's outwardly, when you present yourself outwardly as a
Christian who seems genuine but changes behind
closed doors. Over time an inwardly Chiristian will
see the two-faced Christian.

Do not let sin reign your mortal body (Romans
6:12). Sin is death. Your mortal body is already dead
because of sin. If the Spirit who has raised Jesus lives
in us, we have eternal life (Romans 8:11). His Spirit
lives in us.

People showed me love, mercy, compassion, for-giveness, and thankfulness. Have you ever watched ripples in the water? Think of all the love, mercy, compassion, forgiveness, and thankfulness all reaching out in continuous movement. It ripples all over the world. Our mortal bodies become happy, joyful, and grateful for the kindness someone has shown to us.

Our mortal bodies will have life-threatening trials, not just physical but spiritual, sinful trials that hurt our mortal bodies.

2 Corinthians 4:11
For we who are alive are always being given over
to death for Jesus' sake, so that his life may also be
revealed in our mortal body.

Weeping

Revelation 5:4
I wept and wept because no one was found who was
worthy to open the scroll or look inside.

HAVE YOU EVER REACHED A POINT WHEN
all you want to do is weep because too many hur-
dles seem to come at you all at once? I have felt like
that way too many times. When I got to the point
of weeping again, I went to the bible to see who all
was weeping.

John weeps from a vision he received about the
future (Revelation 5:4). He was fearful when he saw
no one was worthy to open the scroll. Then an elder
said "Do not weep!" John saw the Lion. the root
of David, then he saw the Lamb looking as if it had
been slain (Revelation 5:5-6).

Jesus is the only worthy one who is able to open
the scroll. He came to save the world from sin. When
he died, our sins died too. He came to forgive us
our sins. He sacrificed his blood for us. He is the

Lamb. "The Son of Man must be delivered over to the hands of sinners, be crucified and on the third day be raised again" (Luke 24:7).

Just visualize yourself in front of God, standing before His throne. You see books are opened. One of the books is the book of life. You begin to see the dead are judged by what they have done as recorded in the books. Then you see death is thrown into the lake of fire (Revelation 20:11-15). You begin to weep because you know the final judgement is upon you. You weep! Are you scared? Are you not ready? This weeping is an eye opener!

John 5:29

Those who have done what is good will rise to live, and those who have done what is evil will rise to be condemned.

Made in Heaven

Psalm 139:14
I praise you because I am fearfully and wonderfully
made; your works are wonderful, I know that full well.

WHEN YOU'RE CURIOUS ABOUT WHERE
something is made, you'll usually look at the tag,
especially if you like the quality of how it feels, works,
and looks.

Right now I'm enjoying sparkles on my baseball
caps. For some odd reason I want to know where
they are made, so I look. All are made in China
except for one, which is made in Vietnam. They
are all different in how they feel and how they fit
on my head.

Since my hair has a lot of gray now, I'm into sparkles to let my gray stand out. I'm proud to show my
natural gray. I have learned and accomplished a lot
in my years.

In the beginning God created heaven and the
earth (Genesis 1:1). God made every living creature,

the stars, light, man and woman. We are created in our mother's womb the way God created us in His own eyes. I have my own personal birthmark that no one else has. We are made in heaven. God knew who I was before I was created from birth, He knows me now, and will know me till I die. He created me just the way I am. It took me some years to see how I am able to display His glory in myself.

Ephesians 1: 6,14
To the praise of his glorious grace, which he has freely given us in the One he loves. Who is a deposit guaranteeing our inheritance until the redemption of those who are God's possession—to the praise of his glory.

My Grief

Jeremiah 10:19
Woe to me because of my injury! My wound is incurable! Yet I said to myself, "This is my sickness, and I must endure it."

THIS GRIEF FEELS LIKE I MYSELF AM DYING on the inside. It is a lonely feeling only I am experiencing. It can't be put into words. It is different from depression. I myself have a heavy loss. I'm not able to do what I once could do on my own. I'm too young to have to rely on my son and his fiancé to help me. My concussion took a downturn. At times this gives me grievance.

In Jeremiah 10:19, the keywords are "I must endure it." I retreat back to my quiet place for Spiritual renewal. I don't need to be on any more medicine to avoid getting too deep in my personal grief. I need to overcome it. With spring here, I look beyond my situation with acceptance along with new growth of the trees and the new flower buds about to open. Next spring will be an all-new season to look forward to. I'll see the changes and some improvements in this situation along with the new flower buds that will also bloom.

Zephaniah 3:17
"The Lord your God is with you, the Mighty Warrior who saves. He will take great delight in you; in his love he will no longer rebuke you, but will rejoice over you with singing."

Jeremiah and Me

Jeremiah 12:2-3
You have planted them, and they have taken root: they grow and bear fruit. You are always on their lips but far from their hearts. Yet you know me Lord...

I SEE "BUT FAR FROM THEIR HEARTS" AS someone who pretends to show care and concern. Their heart is actually the opposite of any kind of care. They are the smooth-talking false people, the false prophets. It isn't just the wicked people in Jeremiah's time who Jeremiah wanted to question God about in terms of justice.

The wicked have taken root. They have spread, prospered, and continue to bear fruit. When you personally see so much wrong with how the false people present themselves, how they seem to flourish more than the truly good people who have genuine caring hearts. It didn't take me long to see a false bishop on the television when he said, "That is where I think the bible is wrong." My mouth dropped.

When I see falsehood, I distance myself from it or stop watching the television. Like Jeremiah, I also reached out to God. I've even asked God "why," but in the end all I could do was pray for the people.

Matthew 7:15
Watch out for false prophets. They come to you in sheep's clothing, but inwardly they are ferocious wolves.

Hebrew 4:13
Nothing in all creation is hidden from God's sight. Everything is uncovered and laid bare before the eyes of him to whom we must give account.

Jigsaw Puzzles

Jeremiah 29:11
"For I know the plans I have for you," declares the Lord, "plans to prosper you and not to harm you, plans to give you hope and a future.

I LOVE JIGSAW PUZZLES. AS I SIT THERE AT the beginning of a 1,000-piece puzzle, I wonder, "How long this will take me?" All I see are lots of pieces that need to fit in the right way. There have been a few 1,000-piece puzzles that have taken me three days to complete, and some took even longer.

Pieces of life are like a jigsaw puzzle. The job you got laid off from—that piece didn't fit. When you move from your home you thought was a forever home—that piece didn't fit. The time I bought a fern for the second time and it still died in a new place in my yard—that piece didn't fit.

From big pieces to little pieces, what doesn't fit God's plan won't fit your plans. The picture of God's perfect fit for the life He is leading you on means we have to listen to see where He is leading us in this colorful life.

Life is like a jigsaw puzzle—what fits in your life, who fits in your life. Who, what, and where are the bright pieces that will finish this puzzle we call life.

---

1 Thessalonians 5:18
Give thanks in all circumstances; for this is God's will for you in Christ Jesus.

Leaving My Comfort Zone

Luke 9:62
Jesus replied, "No one who puts a hand to the plow
and looks back is fit for service in the kingdom of God."

MY HOUSE AND BACKYARD WERE MY
bubble. A new neighbor moved in next door. It
took about a year before we spoke. Thanks to her, I
moved out of my bubble I created to avoid people.
I cannot look back. I must move forward.

The disciples were with Jesus, got scared, and
woke Jesus when strong winds came. Jesus calmed
the water (Mark 4:35-41). Turbulent water is scary.
I've been on choppy waters while the boat was
moving to where we were wanting to go, which was
across to the other side of the lake. I kept thinking,
"Is the boat going to stay together? Am I going to
bounce out of it?" I would hold fast to my son who
was in elementary school at the time. We always
made it back safely. Through traumatic, turbulent,
and stressful times, you will overcome to see the

beauty that follows. Without the turbulent water, the pretty seashells wouldn't wash up on the shores.

Proverbs 31:30
Charm is deceptive, and beauty is fleeting; but a woman who fears the Lord is to be praised.

God's Anger

KARAH, DATHAN, AND ABIRAM (NUMBERS 16) are examples of what God did when rebellion and grumbling didn't stop. When I read, "the ground under them split apart and the earth opened its mouth and swallowed them and their households.." (Numbers 16:31-34), my stomach dropped—not in a bad way, but in a "Oh my!" kind of way. It's not just the Book of Numbers that shows how God's anger is not like ours. Jesus came and calmed God's anger. He is slow to anger, it seems at times very slow to anger, when hearts continue to be evil and wicked. God holds off His anger. He's offering repentance (2 Peter 3:9).

It's an evil person that uses someone much younger as a spy or informer. The younger person may be very influenced by the older person. The older person may take advantage of the younger person and use the younger person to his advantage. This is what I call deceitful. It's sad to see. All you can do is pray and pray. What's the reason? What's the purpose? What's the motive? Look at Jude 16. It's the final set of character traits of the ungodly. Jude is a very small book worth reading.

Jude 16

These people are grumblers and faultfinders; they follow their own evil desires; they boast about themselves and flatter others for their own advantage.

Staying Connected

Colossians 1:16-17
For in him all things were created: things in heaven
and on earth, visible and invisible, whether thrones or
powers or rulers or authorities; all things have been created through him and for him. He is before all things,
and in him all things hold together.

WHEN BOTH PEOPLE IN A COUPLE WORK,
there isn't enough time for each other. After a while
couples need time to themselves to stay connected.
God feels the same way. He wants to spend one-
on-one time with you.

In Colossians 1:16-17 you read "all things" four
times. All things visible and invisible. The creator of
the universe wants His one-on-one time with each
individual person. Remember, He knows how many
hairs we have (Matthew 10:30; Luke 12:7). God
knows every star (Isaiah 40:26).

When you don't spend one-on-one time with
God, you become more distant from Him. Over

thirty years together with my husband, we keep learning new things about each other. Marriage, relationships, and raising a family can have rough spots—so can our walk with Jesus.

I'm over fifty, but I still continue to learn about life. Each day and each year there is always something to learn. As I continue to grow spiritually, my discovering of our savior will be a lifelong process. The bible has so much learning and so much new discovering. It all says something good as I walk. After all, what happens here on earth is not eternity. Jesus will lead you to your eternal rest.

Jeremiah 9:24
"But let the one who boasts boast about this: that they have the understanding to know me, that I am the Lord, who exercises kindness, justice and righteousness on earth, for in these I delight."

On Bended Knees

Daniel 6:10

Now when Daniel learned that the decree had been published, he went home to his upstairs room where the windows opened toward Jerusalem. Three times a day he got down on his knees and prayed, giving thanks to his God, just as he had done before.

DANIEL CONTINUED TO PRAY AFTER THE published decree. After he prayed for his thankfulness, Daniel also needed God's wisdom for the kingdom (Daniel 6:3). Despite the obstacles that lay ahead of him, Daniel never lost his faith. I prayed many times on my knees. There's a feeling I get that makes me stop what I'm doing to go to my room, get on my knees, and begin to pray about what has come to me until I feel better. Then I can go about my day.

I have a picture of George Washington kneeling in prayer at Valley Forge. He had to go off alone with a strong urge to kneel down on his knees and pray to God. His faith in God was well known.

Samuel anoints David as king (1 Samuel 16). David took refuge in a cave (Psalm 142). Like David took refuge in a cave, George Washington took refuge away from camp in that terrible winter of 1777-1778 to be one-on-one with God in prayer. One became the chosen king of Israel by God. The other became known as one of the founding fathers of the United States.

Psalm 142:3

When my spirit grows faint within me, it is you who watch over my way. In the path where I walk.

I Feel the Need

John 13:13
You call me 'Teacher' and 'Lord' and rightly so, for
that is what I am.

I FEEL THE NEED TO COME TO MY DESK TO
study and write, and at times I feel a very strong
need to get down on my knees and pray.

I purchased an old teacher's bell—solid brass
with a real wooden handle. I can look at this bell
and wonder what my teacher has for me today. My
teacher is calling me.

I have two teachers I think about even now from
my school days. For me to keep thinking about them
on and off means they made an impact on me. One
teacher in my senior year was my math teacher. I
wasn't doing too well one particular class. If it wasn't
for her going to the other teacher asking him if she
can help me, I would not have graduated with my
class. The other teacher somehow always moved up
each year and happened to be with my class. I had

her from middle school starting in the fifth grade all the way through high school. Before she started class, she always read from a book after roll call. I'll never forget either of these teachers.

Teachers help kids learn reading, writing, mathematics, science, biology, and the list goes on of what teachers do to provide what students need to learn and know in order to succeed when they graduate.

God teaches us how to handle temptations (1 Corinthians 10:13), how to live righteously (Ephesians 4:17-32), and the value of adversity and perseverance (James 1:2-4). Most importantly, He lets us know nothing can separate us from Christ (Romans 8:38-39). Christ's love alone withstands all the world throws at you.

---

2 Timothy 3:14-17
But as for you, continue in what you have learned and have become convinced of, because you know those from whom you learned it, and how from infancy you have known the Holy Scriptures, which are able to make you wise for salvation through faith in Christ Jesus.

Childlike vs Childish

Ephesians 6:4
Fathers, do not exasperate your children; instead bring
them up in the training and instruction of the Lord.

AS I FINISHED A PAGE IN A BOOK I WAS
reading, I realize how much I've wanted to go
deeper in my studies of what it means to be childlike versus childish. Childlike is trusting in God—a
miracle prayer was answered. I realized God's mighty
hand is at work here through my prayer. This is just
one example of childlike faith to trust in the importance of why Jesus came to earth, why he died for
us—not just for forgiveness of sins but to teach us
the way. I'm trusting what I can't see in the spirit. As
my faith grows spiritually, my childlike faith becomes
more dependent on Jesus speaking to God on my
behalf (John 14:6).

I've also had childish faith. I was trusting people
with words of untruth. I continued to believe them
for several years. My childish faith also had me acting

childish at times. As I think back on that, I'm so embarrassed. It sure humbled me.

Childish faith also is when you rush God. It's childish to think you are above any kind of authority. Nobody is above God's law. Manmade laws are meant to protect and serve. We need laws so there will be peace and protection. Without laws this country would be total mayhem, and there would be a lot of deaths with total mayhem.

Childlike faith is trust in God. Childish faith is unbelief and mayhem.

James 4:10
Humble yourselves before the Lord, and he will lift you up.

Chapters of Life

Philippians 1:6
Being confident of this, that he who began a good
work in you will carry it on to completion until the day
of Christ Jesus.

FOR SOME TIME, THE PROBLEMS HERE SEEM
to be like a newsreel on repeat, constantly playing
and replaying the happenings of the past situations
that kept coming and coming and coming. That
chapter was a very intense time in my life. Eventually
some people will stop talking about the past and
replaying the old newsreel drama. If not, then it's
sad to say it may never stop being talked about. This
chapter will be closed by some but won't be for-
gotten, and some will be able to forget the drama
that kept the newsreels going.

Your life is a story with many chapters. Some
chapters come to an end while other chapters are
still opening into the next chapter. Your life story
will either help people or they will live in a state of

unrest. With unrest, the spirit and the soul is also in a state of unrest. My spirit and my soul were living in a state of unrest. Many times I read Hebrews 4:12. Finally it was a wakeup call for me, and it also lifted me up at the same time. I had to work with myself. My Spiritual food is God's Word and my studies of theology. I needed this deeper learning so I could heal Spirituality with my soul.

Hebrews 4:12
For the word of God is alive and active. Sharper than any double-edged sword it penetrates even to dividing soul and spirit, joints, and marrow; it judges the thoughts and attitudes of the heart.

Tarnished Image

1 Peter 3:16
Keeping a clear conscience, so that those who speak
maliciously against your good behavior in Christ may
be ashamed of their slanders.

WHEN YOUR IMAGE IS TARNISHED BY
someone, you know it by people who you have
never spoken to. You see someone in the same line
at the store at the same register. That person has
already pictured the image of you based on what
has been said about in order to tarnish your image.
Well, their plan has worked. Your image is tarnished
to the point the person in line with you won't even
speak to you. You begin to feel uneasy, wondering
why the person keeps glancing at you. In the end
you will learn why.

It seems to make things worse when you defend
yourself from slander. What do you do? The best
thing is to be quiet (Exodus 14:14). Begin to heal
your mind, body, spirit, and soul. Learn to be in

the presence of God (Hebrews 11:6). Refresh your mind with God's words (1 Corinthians 2:9-10). God made it known to the Prophet Isaiah (Isaiah 53:5) how our spiritual wounds in salvation will be healed by Christ's death, as well as in Philippians 2:8-11.

Tarnished images are just evil and are Satan's work. Look at it as offense and defense. Satan is on the offense, you're on the defense. You're in spiritual warfare. When Satan latches onto someone, he's all in. He will continue to wreak havoc in any way, shape, or form he can. When Satan latches on, people become lost sheep. As you are on the defense your warfare is about submitting and letting God have control. As you let God be in control, begin to be alert to your inner feelings and let anger go. Forgiveness needs to happen. Begin to pray for people who have tarnished your image.

Romans 3:24
All are justified freely by his grace through the redemption that came by Jesus Christ.

How I Overcame

Jeremiah 29:11
"For I know the plans I have for you," declares the Lord, "plans to prosper you and not to harm you, plans to give you hope and a future."

IT TAKES COURAGE TO FACE STRUGGLES head on. At times it will be very difficult. It can wreak havoc on your mental state.

First, seek medical help if you need it. Professional help is the first step to healing. God created you and everyone else, and that includes doctors (Ephesians 2:10).

Reach for the bible and begin to seek a good bible church. The word of God never spoils. It is everyday food for eternal life (John 6:27). When you buy food at the grocery store, how often do you have to throw away food that is spoiled? That food feeds your mortal body. If you don't understand the bible, buy books to help, or there are plenty of great television ministries all day every day.

Begin to look around you at what God has already created. The birds don't worry (Matthew 6:26) and the ants already know where to go (Proverbs 6:6-8; 30:24-25). The wind that blows—imagine it is Jesus's breath on you. He is helping you along (John 20:22). Our comfort is truly through Jesus Christ who suffered for us. All we have to do is reach out to him (2 Corinthians 1:5).

---

1 Peter 2:9
But you are a chosen people, a royal priesthood, a holy nation, God's special possession, that you may declare the praises of him who called you out of darkness into his wonderful light.

Study Time

Psalm 111:2
Great are the works of the Lord; they are pondered by
all who delight in them.

PONDERED MEANS THINKING. YOUR learning begins when you read and think. When you think about what you read, your meditation begins. Meditation is the beginning of absorbing God's Word inside you—your food for eternal life has begun.

When the food of God's Word comes deeper inside you, then you'll see the importance of trusting in the Lord is greater than trusting in humans (Psalm 118:8). Humans are emotional. It's our nature to be emotional for good times, celebrations, during illness. There is also emotional eating (I'm guilty). There are many more emotions we go through—too many to be listed. Being emotional seems to be the hardest battle in spiritual warfare when emotions are on the negative side. When depression, anger, low self-esteem, fear, and many more bring you down, keep building yourself up to overcome these emotions. Bring positive thoughts to your mind. Keep your heart cheerful (Proverbs 17:22).

When you focus on and study God's Word, the negative emotions will not stay or linger. If you let it linger, then it latches onto you. Once it latches inside of you, then you become desperate to the point of hopelessness. Study time every day is my key to healing many emotions so they do not linger in me to the point where I become a hopeless mess emotionally.

Isaiah 40:28-29

Do you not know? Have you not heard? The Lord is the everlasting God, the Creator of the ends of the earth. He will not grow tired or weary and his understanding no one can fathom. He gives strength to the weary and increases the power of the weak.

Praise God

Psalm 113:1-3
Praise the Lord. Praise the Lord, you his servants;
praise the name of the Lord. Let the name of the Lord
be praised, both now and forevermore. From the rising
of the sun to the place where it sets, the name of the
Lord is to be praised.

WHEN I BEGAN TO PRAISE GOD MORE, THE worries began to leave and become less frequent. For as long as I praised God, my mind began to slowly move on to God. My worries became God's worries. I felt so desperate for God to end all that kept coming at me. I kept feeling attacked from all directions and was overwhelmed mentally and emotionally.

Psalm 113 reminds us all that God is eternal. His sovereignty is at work. Through my sufferings to my healing to blessing me time and time again.. We have an awesome God who is our redeemer when hard trials end and you begin to see how He has been working with you for His glory and a great testimony. Or it could be the other way around. God could be showing you where you need to make a change. He made a change in me. He will make a change in you

<hr/>

Psalm 113
Praise the Lord.
Praise the Lord, you his servants;
praise the name of the Lord.
Let the name of the Lord be praised,
both now and forevermore.
From the rising of the sun to the place where it sets,
the name of the Lord is to be praised.
The Lord is exalted over all the nations,
his glory above the heavens.
Who is like the Lord our God,
the One who sits enthroned on high,
who stoops down to look
on the heavens and the earth?
He raises the poor from the dust
and lifts the needy from the ash heap;
he seats them with princes,
with the princes of his people.
He settles the childless woman in her home
as a happy mother of children.
Praise the Lord.

<hr/>

Gold

Psalm 19:9-10
The fear of the Lord is pure, enduring forever. The
decrees of the Lord are firm, and all of them are righteous. They are more precious than gold, than much
pure gold; they are sweeter than honey, than honey
from the honeycomb.

THE CALIFORNIA GOLD RUSH COMES TO
mind when the word gold is used or heard. It shaped
the course of California's development. Look at
California today. The most popular pieces of gold
are gold coins. People buy to collect or invest
towards retirement. Jewelry is often made of gold.
Some people lock their jewelry in safes because they
are very expensive pieces.

The first mention of gold is in Genesis 2:10-
12. God is the creator of gold. Gold is mentioned
more than a hundred times in the Bible. God's uses
for gold were for the Ark (Exodus 25:8-22), the
Table (Exodus 25:23-30), the Lampstand (Exodus

25:31-40), and the Tabernacle (Exodus 26:29-37). God's Holy Place was built with gold. God's Tabernacle was a thing of beauty with its colors, acacia wood, cherubim, and the list goes on.

While the Ark was with the family of Obed-Edom in his house, God blessed his household and everything in it (1 Chronicles 13:14). God's law was not a burden to believers when David wrote Psalm 19:9-10. As believers today, we see how still more precious than gold His decrees are. David had statues as his reminders. I have pictures to keep reminding me His Words are sweeter than honeycomb.

As I look at my gold wedding band, my love for my husband is strong. God's love is 100% more for us. You feel His love as He blesses you with unexpected expectations we never dream would happen. The joy and happiness you feel is a joyful one. That's God's love you feel!

Ephesians 2:4-7
But because of his great love for us, God who is rich in mercy, made us alive with Christ even when we were dead in transgressions—-it is by grace you have been saved. And God raised us up with Christ and seated us with him in the heavenly realms in Christ Jesus, in order that in the coming ages he might show the incomparable riches of his grace, expressed in his kindness to us in Christ Jesus.

Resilience

Philippians 4:13
I can do all this through him who gives me strength.

I WAS READING THE NEWSPAPER AND SAW
the word *resilience*. We have been in this COVID-19
pandemic for many months now as I'm writing this
page, with cases continuing to rise. During the lock
down, I was so glad I was able to go to the grocery store at times. More stores and restaurants have
opened back up. There are some whose doors had
to close forever in my area. Resilience is about being
strong. I'll say for me, resilience is being strong mentally in spite of my injury. But there are days where
I'm not able to leave the house at all.

As we live in the present time we need to be
resilient for however long we need to be. You too
can share this blessing of life as you heal from the
trauma of this scary pandemic. You'll be other people's hope as a survivor. Become the positive the
world needs. Being positive will spread throughout

your community. You'll become someone people will look up to so they too will be a positive survivor for others. This positivity is like a domino effect. One positive survivor touches another positive survivor, then that positive survivor touches another positive survivor, and it continues to spread through your community and beyond your community

Become the positive of hope in this world. That hope is the pathway of resilience no matter how suffocating this fear of the pandemic may be. Think of the positive to get you through. Become that first domino that touches someone else.

Ephesians 6:10
Finally, be strong in the Lord and in his mighty power.

Release of My Fears

Mark 6:50

Because they saw him and were terrified. Immediately he spoke to them and said, "Take courage! It is I. Don't be afraid."

As I READ MARK 6:45-51, I'M REMINDED OF what my granddaughter said to me. I have a painting of Jesus walking on the stormy waters with the full moon behind his head. The ship is in the background. One day my granddaughter told me, "that picture scares me." I told her about the meaning of the painting. After I explained it to her she went back to looking for more toys to play with.

It also made me realize my fears have been released from the paralyzing feeling that kept me in the house. When Jesus climbed into the boat, the winds died down (Mark 6:51). That is the feeling I now receive. Jesus took my fear and calmed my Spirit.

My health is also restored from what that fear had caused. My stomach is no longer in knots. My heartbeat feels normal again. The panic attacks with anxiety have slowed down tremendously.

Jesus made history with all his healings and miracles that are written. Rest assured the lord is still healing and performing miracles today.

Romans 8:15
The Spirit you received does not make you slaves, so that you live in the fear again; rather, the Spirit you received brought about your adoption to sonship. And by him we cry, *"Abba,"* Father.

The Aromas

2 Corinthians 2:15-16
For we are to God the pleasing aroma of Christ among
those who are being saved and those who are perishing.
To the one we are an aroma that brings death; to the
other, an aroma that brings life.

THE AROMA OF COFFEE BREWING SPREADS
quickly through a home. You already know someone
is brewing coffee. The aroma of a cake baking—
something sweet for dessert is baking in the oven.
The aroma of herbs in the main dish—you know it's
already going to be tasty. These three examples are
aromas everyone is familiar with. Each one brings
an aroma to your senses. Just think when you add
herbs and spices to food, how it brings taste to the
food so it isn't tasteless.

Through spreading the gospel, the Apostles
spread the knowledge of God Himself through
Christ. The Apostles are the aroma of life, the fra-
grance of Christ (2 Corinthians 4:10-12). For some,

the aroma of life will be death, for others the aroma of life will be life.

With coffee, cake, and herbs, your senses are of the physical form. Your mortal self knows the purpose of each one. With Christ our aroma of death is forgiven through the death and Resurrection of Jesus Christ. Jesus Christ died to give us eternal life—the aroma of life!

Ephesians 5:2
And walk in the way of love, just as Christ loved us and gave himself up for us as a fragrant offering and sacrifice to God.

Bad Dreams

2 Timothy 1:7
For the Spirit God gave us does not make us timid, but
gives us power, love and self-discipline.

A DREAM CAME TO ME INVOLVING THE
ones who moved away. It bothered me and began
to make me paranoid. I began to pray out of fear my
dream might come true. It seemed so real. I prayed
and praised God, wanting it to just be a bad dream.
I'm surprised I keep dreaming of these people. They
used to pop into my dreams all the time. I had a very
good day, a happy ending to a day, and then at bed-
time, pow! I dreamed about them. I couldn't go back
to sleep after that. God has always known my heart.

Satan's work will come to me in dreams at times.
One day those dreams will stop completely. Satan
knows the stress I endured so he still brings them
to me in my dreams.

Several hours later I feel better. I began to
remember God answered my prayers by having them

move away. God won't bring them back to live very close to me and my family again. God answered, and it's a done deal! Psalm 23 is my calming and visual Psalm.

Psalm 23
The Lord is my shepherd, I lack nothing.
He makes me lie down in green pastures,
he leads me beside quiet waters,
he refreshes my soul.
He guides me along the right paths
for his name's sake.
Even though I walk
through the darkest valley,
I will fear no evil,
for you are with me;
your rod and your staff,
they comfort me.
You prepare a table before me
in the presence of my enemies.
You anoint my head with oil;
my cup overflows.
Surely your goodness and love will follow me
all the days of my life,
and I will dwell in the house of the Lord
forever.

Look for Jesus Around You

2 Corinthians 4:10
We always carry around in our body the death of
Jesus, so that the life of Jesus may also be revealed
in our body.

I WAS CHRISTMAS SHOPPING AT WALMART
and was at the self-checkout finishing up. I was also
getting one hundred dollars in cash back. When I
was done with the little machine and debit card, I
somehow forgot all about that money dangling from
the checkout machine. I walked away. A few seconds
later I hear a man yelling, "Ma'am, Ma'am!" I turned
to the voice and he said, "You left your money." It
was still dangling from the machine. I thanked him. I
saw Jesus in him. My mind was elsewhere, but Jesus
was there through that kind man. A stranger stops
to talk with you. You and the stranger both learn of
common interests. You and the stranger leave each
other feeling happy. You saw Jesus in this stranger
for bringing kindness to you.

At the end of Colossians 1:27 Paul wrote, "Christ in you." Jesus says in John 15:4, "Remain in me." Believers have Christ in them, Jesus's branch stays connected.

Galatians 2:20
I have been crucified with Christ and I no longer live, but Christ lives in me. The life I now live in the body, I live by faith in the Son of God, who loved me and gave himself for me.

My Final Say

Romans 8:1-2
Therefore, there is now no condemnation for those
who are in Christ Jesus, because through Christ Jesus
the law of the Spirit who gives life has set you free from
the law of sin and death.

I WAS OUT WATERING THE BACKYARD IN
the month of July of 2012 with the temperature
well above a hundred degrees and no rain in the
forecast. I looked up and saw the only cloud in the
sky. It looked like an angel, then it started to break
apart. I took a picture. Some people say it looks like
the letter J, others say it looks like an angel. I saw
God's heavenly sign showing me He will be with me.
I felt great after seeing His sign. Then dread came
to me—dread that turned into the toughest times
of my life.

Overcoming suffering takes time. I know my
trials and tough times took years to overcome . As I
type up this manuscript my eyes still tear up. There's

still some healing I still need help with. I have also fallen short at times during this journey. I will get there with continued studies (my own therapy) and knowing my small support group is helping along the way. Most importantly, I continue to reach out to God in Jesus's name.

How do you want to appear when it's time for judgment? My truest understanding taught me a very hard but good lesson: When you realize your circle of people has dwindled and become smaller, then you realize it's this world that has let you down, not God.

Psalm 27:1
The Lord is my light and my salvation whom—shall I fear? The Lord is the stronghold of my life—of whom shall I be afraid?

Isaiah 41:13
For I am the Lord your God who takes hold of your right hand and says to you, Do not fear; I will help you.

About the Author

SABRINA IS AN AVID READER AND LEARNER. She continues to take free online courses with the Dallas Theological Seminary. She has also participated in online courses through the Israel Bible Center. She lives in Texas with her husband.

An important bible study tool used in the writing of this book was the *Holman Illustrated Bible Dictionary* (2003). Nashville, TN: Holman Bible Publishers. "Reprinted and used by permission."

CPSIA information can be obtained
at www.ICGtesting.com
Printed in the USA
LVHW091655230121
677074LV00002BA/40

9 781662 804113